BODY WORKS

MY STRETCHY BODY

LIZA FROMER AND FRANCINE GERSTEIN MD
Illustrated by Joe Weissmann

TUNDRA BOOKS

Published in Canada by Tundra Books,
75 Sherbourne Street, Toronto, Ontario M5A 2P9

Published in the United States by Tundra Books of Northern New York,
P.O. Box 1030, Plattsburgh, New York 12901

Library of Congress Control Number: 2010940342

Library and Archives Canada Cataloguing in Publication

Fromer, Liza
    My stretchy body / Liza Fromer and Francine Gerstein ; illustrated by Joe Weissmann.

(Body works)
ISBN 978-1-77049-203-5

    1. Human body – Juvenile literature. 2. Human physiology – Juvenile
literature. 3. Human anatomy – Juvenile literature.
I. Gerstein, Francine II. Weissmann, Joe, 1947- III. Title.
IV. Series: Body works (Toronto, Ont.)

QP37.F768 2011   j612   C2010-907308-8

We acknowledge the financial support of the Government of Canada through the Book
Publishing Industry Development Program (BPIDP) and that of the Government of Ontario
through the Ontario Media Development Corporation's Ontario Book Initiative.
We further acknowledge the support of the Canada Council for the Arts and the Ontario
Arts Council for our publishing program.

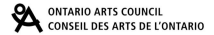

ONTARIO ARTS COUNCIL
CONSEIL DES ARTS DE L'ONTARIO

Medium: watercolor on paper

Design: Leah Springate

Printed and bound in China

1 2 3 4 5 6   16 15 14 13 12 11

Also available in this Body Works series by Liza Fromer and Francine Gerstein MD, illustrated by Joe Weissmann

Authors' Note

The information in this book is to help you understand your body and learn why it works the way it does.

It's important that you see your family doctor at least once each year. If you're worried about your health or think you might be sick, speak to an adult and see your doctor.

Kids are always growing. Parts of your body, like your bones and teeth, stop growing by the time you're an adult. As you get bigger and bigger, so do your muscles – they grow even after your growth spurt stops. Just look at weight lifters – they have really big muscles!

Have you ever wondered why it hurts when you cut your finger, but you don't feel a thing when you cut your hair and nails? When you fall off your bike and skin your knee, it hurts. So why doesn't it hurt when you rub off dry skin? It's because, unlike most other parts of your body, by the time you actually see your hair, nails, and skin, they're already dead. They also keep growing even after the rest of you has stopped. Your body automatically trims off old layers of skin to make way for new ones. These layers are the stretchy parts of your body (MT: integumentary system).

By the way. . .
When you see MT in this book, it stands for Medical Term.

GROWING IS YOUR BODY'S JOB

As a child, one of your body's jobs is to grow. How tall you get depends a lot on your parents' height and whether you eat a healthy, balanced diet. Although you can't really know how tall you'll eventually become, there is a good way to help you guess. Are you curious enough about it to do some math? The Midparental Height calculation will give you a good indication of what your adult height will be.

Boys

- Inches: (Father's Height + Mother's Height + 5 inches) /2 (+ or − 2 inches)
- Centimeters: (Father's Height + Mother's Height + 13 centimeters) /2 (+ or − 5 centimeters)

Girls

- Inches: (Father's Height − 5 inches + Mother's Height) /2 (+ or − 2 inches)
- Centimeters: (Father's Height − 13 centimeters + Mother's Height) /2 (+ or − 5 centimeters)

INSIDE VS. OUTSIDE

It's easy to see what's growing on the outside of your body, but don't forget that your insides are growing along with the rest of you. Your nervous system grows the most in your first two years. When you were a baby, you couldn't do anything for yourself, but by the time you turned two years old, you were walking, talking, feeding yourself, and getting into lots of trouble.

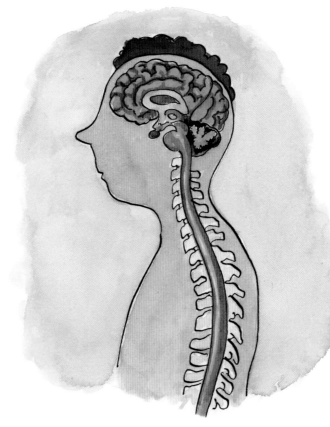

Have you ever noticed that babies' eyes often look bigger than the rest of their faces? Babies are born with almost adult-sized eyeballs. And their heads make up about a quarter of their height.

As of 2009, the tallest man in medical history was Robert Pershing Wadlow, born in Alton, Illinois, in 1918. The last time he was measured, in 1940, he was 8 ft., 11 in. (2.7 m) tall (Guinness World Records). Being that tall requires a lot of bending over — the average door is less than 7 ft. high!

True or false?

If you eat while standing up, your feet will get bigger.
(*False.* And it's more relaxing to sit down while you're eating.)

Doctor says:

"The hypothalamus and the pituitary gland in your brain are responsible for sending out the message to grow."

HAIR

You may not realize this, but your body is covered in hair, except for the palms of your hands, the soles of your feet, and your lips. So why don't you look as hairy as a gorilla or a bear? Well, the hairs on your body are different shapes and sizes. Hair on your head can be thick and long. Hair on your arms and legs is thin and short. And hair on your face is often the thinnest and shortest of all. In fact, it's so fine that some people call it peach fuzz. (Of course, men can grow long beards and mustaches, if they want.)

These days, the hair on your head is mainly just there to look nice, but that hasn't always been the case. Hair used to have a more important job. A long time ago, our ancestors lived in caves without heat. Their hair helped them to stay warm and protected their heads from the sun. Your eyebrows and eyelashes still have a pretty big job: eyebrows keep salty sweat from dripping into your eyes, and eyelashes keep out dirt and dust.

Each hair in your skin grows from a tiny tube (MT: hair follicle). New hair cells are made at the bottom of the tube, and, as they grow, they push the older hair cells up and out of the tube. The cells are full of keratin, a waxy substance that flattens, hardens,

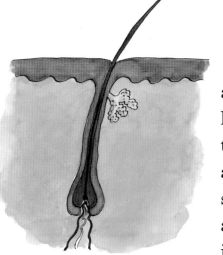

and sticks the cells together, forming a strand of hair – so every strand is a quilt of hair cells stuck to one another! The strand of hair grows longer as it's pushed up the follicle to the surface of your skin. And only the base or root of the strand is alive. Hair has a growing phase (MT: anagen), an in-between or transitional phase (MT: catagen), and a resting or falling-out phase (MT: telogen). The average person has about 100,000 hair follicles on their head. Every day, fifty to a hundred hairs fall out. (You'll see them on your hairbrush.) Luckily, not all the hairs on your head go through this phase at the same time!

#1 Animals that shed their fur (another word for hair) have follicles that go through the growth phase at the same time. That's why your dog or cat may leave a lot of hair behind on your couch in the spring.

#2 The length of your hair depends on the length of its growth phase. Hair on your head has a growth phase that lasts two to seven years, so it can get very long. Hair on your arms and legs has a growth phase that lasts only two months, so it stays short.

True or False?

Your scalp has the largest number of hair follicles on your body. (*False.* Your forehead does.)

SKIN

Skin is your body's armor. It protects you from infection by keeping out dirt, germs, and other yucky particles. Skin is made up of two layers: the inner layer (MT: dermis) and the outer layer (MT: epidermis), both of which are made up of other tiny layers.

Skin helps to ensure that you don't get too hot or too cold. If you have extra body heat, for example, you can get rid of it by sweating. And the dermis has its own set of blood vessels that help control your body temperature. If you're too cold, the blood vessels constrict to keep in heat; but if you're too hot, these blood vessels expand so that there are more places in the vessel walls for heat to escape. Think about a cup of hot chocolate. If the cup has a lid with a tiny hole, there's only a small area for the heat to escape (just like the vessels when they constrict). But if you take off the lid, your delicious hot chocolate will cool down much faster because the heat has a lot more room to escape (just like when your blood vessels expand).

Even when you're sleeping, there's lots of work going on right beneath your skin. New cells are constantly being made at the bottom of the epidermis

that push the older skin cells upward. These older cells flatten and fill with keratin, which makes them strong and hard. As the cells flatten, they die, rise to the surface of the skin, and flake off (MT: desquamate). This whole process takes around twenty-eight days.

The skin has special sensors that react to touch, pain, heat, cold, and pressure. There are also special pigment cells (MT: melanocytes) in the dermis that produce melanin to help protect your skin from the sun's strong rays. Without these cells, you would burn more easily. And, have you ever heard of vitamin D? Well, you can thank your skin for making it for the rest of your body to use. Can you believe that your skin is so busy?

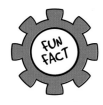

Skin is the body's largest organ, weighing around 3 kilograms (7 pounds) in an average-sized adult.

True or False?

Most of the dust in our homes is made of dead skin cells. (*True.* Sounds gross, doesn't it?)

Doctor says:

"Your skin makes vitamin D, but it needs the help of sunlight. One of vitamin D's jobs is to provide your bones with calcium. Without enough vitamin D and calcium, your bones won't grow properly."

NAILS

Nails protect your fingers and toes. They help you pick up small objects, peel things, and scratch your itchy parts.

Your fingernails and toenails are made of many parts. The hard nail you see is the nail plate; the skin underneath it is the nail bed; the skin that surrounds your nail is the nail fold; and the light-colored half-moon at the bottom of your nail is the lunula. All of these parts work together to create a healthy nail.

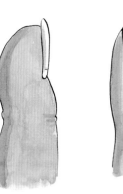

Just like your hair and skin, only the root (MT: matrix) of your nail is alive. Most of the root hides under the skin, at the base of your nail fold. The only part of the root you can actually see is the lunula. The root produces nail cells, which, like hair and skin cells, are full of keratin. As more and more cells are made in the root, the older ones are pushed out and flattened into a strong hard nail.

FUN FACTS

#1 As of 2009, Lee Redmond held the record for the longest fingernails in the world. Her longest nail measured 2 ft. 11 in. (89 cm) (Guinness World Records). It must have taken her days to polish them!

#2 Fingernails take three to six months to regrow completely, but toenails take twelve to eighteen months.

True or False?

Although most people have flesh-colored nails, some people are born with shiny red or pink nails. (*False*. But if it were true, it sure would save people a lot of money on nail polish.)

Doctor says:

"Don't pick the skin around your nails. Tearing the cuticle can cause bleeding and infection. Some people call the piece of loose skin that hangs from the side of the nail a hangnail. As tempting as it may be to pick it off, ask your parents to help you remove it gently with a nail clipper."

GROWING MUSCLES

Now you know that most parts of your body grow by adding more cells. But your muscles grow in a different way. They are made up of little fibers, and the number of muscle fibers that you have is determined by genetics (all the stuff your parents pass on to you). In order for your muscles to grow, a message is sent from your brain along your nerves to your muscles. Muscles move your joints by contracting – pulling one end of the muscle closer to the other end.

Exercise and nutrition also play a big part in how your muscles grow. As you grow, so do your muscles. But that doesn't mean that you get more muscles; it means the muscles that you do have get bigger and stronger. Whenever you exercise, stress is put on your muscles, causing tiny injuries (MT: micro-injuries) to the muscle fibers. When you rest, your muscles repair themselves. They need to get stronger to protect themselves for the next round of exercise. And the more often you exercise, the stronger your muscle fibers will be. No matter how young or old you are, your muscles get bigger with activity and smaller with inactivity.

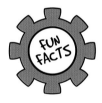

#1 The biggest muscle in your body is the gluteus maximus, found in each of your buttocks.

#2 The smallest muscle in your body is the stapedius, deep in each ear. It's attached to the smallest bone in your body, the stapes or stirrup.

True or False?

You have more than 600 muscles in your body. (*True.*)
There are ten muscles in your face. (*False.* There are over fifty muscles!)

Doctor says:

"Your muscles are made of three-quarters water."

GROWING BONES

There are different types of bones in your body: long bones like the ones in your legs, short bones that you'd find in your wrists, flat bones that make up part of your hips, and more. A bone is made up of different parts. The outer surface of a bone (MT: periosteum) is like plastic wrap. The next layer down is compact bone, which forms a hard smooth shell.

A bone may seem hard, but its center is actually a mixture of spongy bone (MT: cancellous bone) and red or yellow marrow, which is like jelly. Red marrow makes blood cells; yellow marrow is simply fat.

Your bones are a lot different from your parents' bones. Your bones have growth plates – little spaces that are full of soft cartilage that helps them grow. In order for you to grow, the cartilage in your growth plates must grow. When the cartilage has grown, it breaks down and is replaced by new bone. This process continues until your late teens or early twenties, when the cartilage stops growing and your growth plates turn to bone. This means you've stopped growing. Bone growth is controlled by special products (MT: hormones) that are made by your body.

At night, your legs may feel sore and achy. You may hear the term "growing pains," but growing bones don't really hurt, and you can't actually feel them growing. What you feel is likely muscle pain caused by overuse (running, jumping, and climbing) during the day. A heating pad or a little leg massage from your parents may make you feel better.

#1 Babies are born with around 300 bones in their bodies. Some of these bones fuse together and some don't, so by the time you're an adult, you have only 206 bones.

#2 Although your bones technically stop growing when you're an adult, it doesn't mean they stop working. Even when adults fall and break a bone, their bodies repair the area by creating new bone.

True or False?

Most birds have many hollow bones that make them light enough to fly. (*True.* The number of bones depends on the type of bird.)

GROWING TEETH

You have different teeth to do different jobs: your incisors cut your food, your canines tear your food, your premolars tear and crush it, and your molars grind it up. And although you can see some parts of your teeth, there are others you can't see. You can see the crown and the white enamel that covers your teeth, but you can't see the root, the dentin, or the pulp. The pulp holds the nerves and blood vessels.

A few months after you were born, your baby teeth started to grow in (MT: tooth eruption). It was painful because they had to tear through your gums in order to come out. Typically, humans have twenty baby teeth (MT: primary teeth) and thirty-two adult teeth (MT: permanent teeth). Usually, your first two teeth are the lower incisors, with all the rest arriving by the

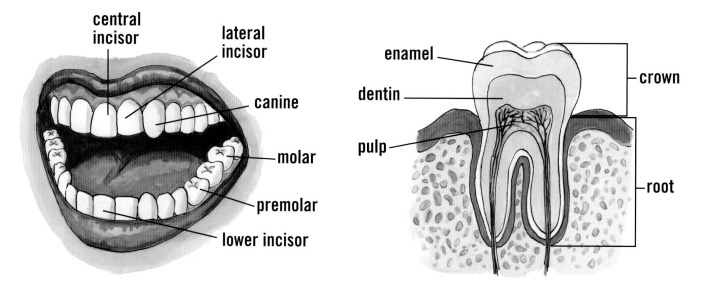

time you're two or three years old. Your adult teeth usually grow in by the time you're eleven or twelve. So if it hurts when your baby teeth grow in, why doesn't it hurt when they fall out? Well, if you don't try to wiggle them out before they're ready, the adult teeth just push them out.

Although baby teeth are only in your mouth temporarily, they have very important jobs. They reserve space for your permanent teeth; they help you pronounce words correctly; they help you chew your food; and they make you look nice when you smile. If you don't take care of your baby teeth, they can decay or become infected, which could lead to problems with your adult teeth, waiting right below them. The main reasons for losing adult teeth (you really don't want to lose those if you can help it!) are decay and gum disease, so take care of your teeth by brushing, flossing, not eating too much candy, and getting regular checkups at the dentist.

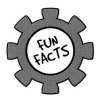

#1 Candy is bad for your teeth because it has sugar in it. When sugar sits on your teeth, it changes to acid, which causes tooth decay.

#2 Elephants have the biggest teeth. In fact, elephant tusks are actually enormous incisors.

True or False?

White chocolate is better for your teeth than milk chocolate because it's the same color as your teeth. (*False.* But nice try!)

Isn't it amazing what your growing body can do!

Glossary

Calcium, cartilage, genetics, growth spurt, hormones, joints, muscle fibers, nervous system, pigment, sensors.

Calcium: A mineral that is found mainly in the hard part of your bones. It's required for heart, nerve, and muscle function.

Cartilage: Fibrous connective tissue found in different parts of the body, such as the joints and the outer ear.

Genetics: The study of inherited characteristics in related organisms. For example, you may have long arms like your mother and curly hair like your father.

Growth spurt: A period of rapid increase in height, weight, and muscle mass occurring in adolescence.

Hormones: Products of living cells that stimulate activity in other cells of the body.

Joints: The areas where one bone comes into contact with another bone for the purpose of moving body parts.

Muscle fibers: Cells that make up muscles.

Nervous system: A complex information-processing system, which consists of the brain, spinal cord, and nerves.

Pigment: A substance that gives color to skin and hair.

Sensors: Respond to physical stimuli, such as light, pressure, heat, and sound.